LIFE IN ABUNDANCE

*G*rowing in Hope

◆ ◆ ◆ ◆ ◆

LIFE IN ABUNDANCE

Growing in Hope

by
Lou Anne M. Tighe

Saint Mary's Press
Christian Brothers Publications
Winona, Minnesota

Genuine recycled paper with 10% post-consumer waste. Printed
with soy-based ink.

The publishing team included Carl Koch, development editor;
Laurie A. Berg, copy editor; James H. Gurley, production editor
and typesetter; Maurine R. Twait, art director; pre-press, printing,
and binding by the graphics division of Saint Mary's Press.

The acknowledgments continue on page 90.

Printed in the United States of America

Printing: 9 8 7 6 5 4 3 2 1

Year: 2006 05 04 03 02 01 00 99 98

ISBN 0-88489-385-5

◆ ◆ ◆ ◆ ◆

to *Helen and Louis*
Victoria and Thomas

Love is the foundation
of hope.

Contents

◆ ◆ ◆ ◆ ◆

Foreword

Jesus said, . . . "I came that [you] may have life,
and have it abundantly."

(John 10:7–10)

Jesus' mission is accomplished in each one of us when we
nourish the seeds of full life that God has planted in the
garden of our soul.

The following story suggests where the task of nurturing the seeds of abundant life needs to begin:

> "I was a revolutionary when I was young and all my
> prayer to God was 'Lord, give me the energy to
> change the world.'
>
> "As I approached middle age and realized that
> half my life was gone without my changing a single
> soul, I changed my prayer to 'Lord, give me the
> grace to change all those who come in contact with
> me. Just my family and friends, and I shall be
> satisfied.'
>
> "Now that I am an old man and my days are
> numbered, my one prayer is, 'Lord, give me the
> grace to change myself.' If I had prayed for this right
> from the start I should not have wasted my life."

(Bayazid)

Jesus made this point much more saliently: "'Why do
you see the speck in your neighbor's eye, but do not
notice the log in your own eye? . . . Take the log out of
your own eye, and then you will see clearly to take the
speck out of your neighbor's eye'" (Matthew 7:3–5).

The meaning of Bayazid's story and Jesus' words is
clear: we live life abundantly when we grow in the qualities of character that make life good. These qualities are
traditionally called virtues—the inner readiness to do
good.

8

Three Brilliant Flowers: Faith, Hope, Love

In the garden of the soul, faith, hope, and love form the centerpiece. They are essential for living abundantly, living fully. Traditionally called theological virtues, they come as free gifts from God and draw us to God. We cannot earn these qualities; God has already freely planted them in us.

Even so, faith, hope, and love need tending. In prayer we can open our heart, mind, and will to God's grace. We embrace and open ourselves to this grace through reflection and conversation with God about what we believe, how we hope, and the ways we love. When we ponder the Scriptures and examine our beliefs, we nourish faith. When we meditate on the goodness of God's creation, on friendships, and on all God's gifts to us, we nourish hope. When we pray for loved ones, consider how we love, empathize with those needing love, and celebrate the love given to us, we nourish love. As faith, hope, and love spread and grow in the garden of our soul, we truly live life abundantly.

A Harvest of Plenty

The good life of faith, hope, and love is further nurtured as we develop the virtues of courage, joy, justice, prudence, moderation, temperance, forgiveness, and so on. Saint Augustine and other spiritual teachers maintained that these virtues are expressions of faith, hope, and especially love. For instance, in the face of danger to a loved one, people find courage that they never dreamed they had. Living prudently—figuring out what is right in a given situation—becomes easier when love reigns in our heart and focuses our will.

Paradoxically, we find that as we grow in the moral virtues, we also nourish faith, hope, and love in ourselves.

For example, as we grow in justice, we begin to look out for the well-being of other people. In short, we grow more loving. Temperance—creating harmony within ourselves—fosters hopefulness.

Growing a Destiny

Growing abundant life means that we change ourselves by changing the small assertions of self, namely our acts, beginning with an act of prayer. The following wise adage provides a helpful way of thinking about how we can grow in abundance:

> Plant an act; reap a habit.
> Plant a habit; reap a virtue or vice.
> Plant a virtue or vice; reap a character.
> Plant a character; reap a destiny.

Developing our character and our destiny begins with the acts that we plant each day, whether we do them consciously or unconsciously. We give shape to our life by each action we take, day by day. A regular pattern of actions becomes a habit. Eventually our habits determine the shape of our character.

Our character is the combination of our virtues and vices. Our destiny is what finally becomes of us, which depends on the character we build in response to God's grace. A Christlike destiny—life in abundance—begins forming with every act of moral virtue. When we pray to be just, temperate, or moderate, when we pray for courage, honesty, and a forgiving spirit, we acknowledge our dependence on God's grace, but we also give our attention to the development of these qualities of character. Praying for moral virtue is planting, weeding, and watering virtuous acts. The harvest of such prayer will be life lived to the full.

We change the world by changing the small part of it that we are. An old adage says: "Prayer does not change things. Prayer changes people, and people change things." Prayer brings us to the God of love who wants us to have a good life, to live fully, to love, to believe, and to hope. If we open ourselves to God's grace, we will change. Then we can change things.

Praying for Life in Abundance

Virtue, like a garden, fails to thrive without attention and care. Prayer tends the garden. It also allows us to ask for forgiveness so that we can start again when we have left the garden untended. The loving God is always waiting to sustain us and to draw us back to full life. Our God is the God of Hosea who says about sinful and ungrateful Israel: "'I led them with cords of human kindness, with bands of love. I was to them like those who lift infants to their cheeks. I bent down to them and fed them'" (11:4).

Living abundantly leads us frequently to turn the care of the world over to God and to take care of our own soul. To deal with his tendency toward harshness, Vincent de Paul told one of his friends: "I turned to God and earnestly begged him to convert this irritable and forbidding trait of mine. I also asked for a kind and amiable spirit." Vincent's movement of heart toward God involved a surrender to God's presence and power. Vincent knew that living like Christ and clothing himself in Christ's virtues—living abundantly—had to begin with knowledge of his own sins and blessings. Times of prayer, the honest opening and offering of ourselves to God, provide the context for a change of heart, mind, and will to happen.

Praying for the virtues of full life may be roughly compared to tending a garden. "It was a great delight for me," writes Teresa of Ávila, "to consider my soul as a garden and reflect that the Lord was taking a walk in it." Prayer—the celebration of gratefulness for the goodness in life—invites God to walk in our garden. Prayer welcomes the Master Gardener to plant the seed of virtue within us. Prayer prepares the soil for the seed when it opens our fears, doubts, sins, and goodness to the gaze and grace of the Creator.

In the Epistle to the Ephesians, Paul tells the community to put on God's armor:

> Be strong in . . . the strength of [God's] power. . . . Take up the whole armor of God. . . . Fasten the belt of truth around your waist, and put on the breastplate of righteousness. As shoes for your feet put on whatever will make you ready to proclaim the gospel of peace. With all of these, take the shield of faith.
>
> (6:10–16)

To help us clothe ourselves in the armor of virtue necessary for a full life, the prayers in this book follow an ancient pattern: listen *(lectio)*, reflect *(meditatio)*, and respond *(oratio)*. Here are some suggestions for using the prayers:

Listen. Each prayer begins with a passage from the word of God, the wisdom of a spiritual writer, or a story. Read the passage attentively at least once, or better yet, several times. Concentrate on one or two sentences that touch your heart; ponder their meaning for you and their effect on you. This type of listening is called *lectio divina*, or "divine studying." The passages are intended to inspire, challenge, or remind you of some essential aspect of the virtue.

Reflect. Once you have listened to wisdom, each prayer invites you to reflect on your own experience. This is *meditatio,* or "paying attention." Each reflection can help you attend to how God has been speaking to you in your past and present experience. If you keep a journal, you may want to write your reflections in it. Take the reflection questions with you as you go about your day; ponder them while you drive, wait for an appointment, prepare for bed, or find any moment of quiet.

Respond. Each reflection ends with a prayer of petition and thanks. In *oratio* we ask God for the help we need in nurturing the virtue that helps to form a good life. We should never be shy in asking God for help. After all, Jesus tells us many times to seek God's grace, and he assures us that God's help will come. Indeed, the word *prayer* means "to obtain by entreaty." The petitionary prayer reminds us that we are truly dependent on the goodness and love of God for developing the virtue. The response prayer usually gives thanks for the gifts God has showered upon us already. Giving thanks is another way of waking us up to all the wonders of God's love.

Try reading the prayers aloud. They gain a different feel and power. Or use one line as a prayer throughout the day. Plant the prayer line in your heart as you repeat it while having a cup of coffee, washing your hands, or sitting at your desk.

Starting Points

Create a sacred space. Jesus said, "'When you pray, go to your private room, shut yourself in, and so pray to your [God] who is in that secret place, and your [God]

who sees all that is done in secret will reward you'"
(Matthew 6:6). Solitary prayer is best done in a place
where you can have privacy and silence, both of which
can be luxuries in the life of a busy person. If privacy and
silence are not possible, create a quiet, safe place within
yourself, perhaps while riding to and from work, sitting
at the dentist's office, or waiting for someone. Do the
best you can, knowing that a loving God is present every-
where.

Move into sacred time. All of time is suffused with
God's presence. So remind yourself that God is present
as you begin your prayer. If something keeps intruding
during your prayer, spend some time talking with God
about it. Be flexible, because God's spirit blows where it
will. Gerald May speaks to this when he says:

> The present . . . contains everything that is
> needed for lovingly beginning the next moment; it
> seeks only our own willing, responsive presence,
> just here, just now. . . . There are no exceptions—
> not in physical pain, not in psychiatric disorder or
> emotional agony, not in relational strife. . . . Love
> is too much with us for there to be any exceptions.

Come to prayer with an open mind, heart, and will.
Trust that God hears you and wants to support your desire to nourish the virtues of a good life. Prayer strength-
ens our will to act. Through prayer God can touch our
will and empower us to live according to what we know
is true.

Prayer is essential to creating life in abundance
because it nourishes the seeds of virtue that are planted
in our soul. Listening to wisdom fertilizes the seed. Reflecting on or attending to the virtue waters the seed.
Responding with petitionary and thanksgiving prayers
shines light on the seed. After reflecting and praying

14

about hope, you will have planted the seed in rich soil so that it can grow. As it grows it will become a bright flower in the garden of your soul.

God be with you as you grow in hope and in living life to the full. You will be a power for the good of us all.

CARL KOCH
Editor

Introduction

Time to Grow

When a person has shoveled a foot of snow off the driveway, tried to pull the car keys from a pocket with heavy mittens on, and waited for the bus in windchills down to fifty degrees below zero, it is difficult to remember that underneath the snow and ice in the frozen ground are billions of seeds. Waiting.

Throughout the winter these seeds lay in the earth as if dead, and they can be easily forgotten. Yet in the spring, some of the seeds will grow into seedlings and flowers. Some of the seeds will become food for birds. Some of the seeds will become weeds to choke off other plants, and some of the seeds will remain in the earth as nutrients for the life of other seeds. When the earth is white with snow and the ground is hard, seeds are waiting there for their time to grow.

Tiny Seeds of Hope

Spiritual writers have often compared the human heart to the soil, and the seeds are grace planted by God. Just as seeds sprout and break through the earth, so too grace-infused human action brings fresh, nurturing life. Grace-full habits of action eventually become virtues. This book of meditations is about nurturing the tiny seed of hope, a quality indispensable to living life to the full.

Christian revelation teaches that the seed of hope is planted in the human heart by God through Jesus Christ's own life, death, and Resurrection. In the sacred mystery of his life and with the Holy Spirit, the seed of hope given by God is revealed in the hope-filled actions of human beings engaged in every season.

16

Images of Hope

While the images of seed and soil help us to understand the presence of hope in the human heart, other images of hope name and describe its attributes. Hope has been described as the energy within us that impels us to a happy ending. It has been called the provision needed for a long journey. Hope is like a harness or yoke for the life journey that joins together the present with the future. Comparing hope to members of the animal kingdom, it is like a lion who rules the forest of calamity and, according to psychologist Erich Fromm, a crouched tiger "which will jump only when the moment for jumping has come."

Hope also has been called a sure and steadfast anchor of the soul (Hebrews 6:19), and a little sister who hides between the skirts of her two older sisters, faith and love. While these are only several of the images of hope, they metaphorically define the virtue of hope as an unflinching, bold, and persistent capacity in the present moment to seize a future that is possible yet unseen.

Erich Fromm describes hope as the readiness "at every moment for that which is not yet born, and yet not become desperate if there is no birth in our lifetime." Hope is the peculiar human ability to transcend the present and its limitations, a fundamental openness to new possibilities because the present time, whether characterized as a time of prosperity or catastrophe, is not the only reality. To assess one's present circumstances with hope is to look on life in its pregnancy—what might come from those situations as they unfold into the future. Hope is the transcendent capacity in every human being that, assisted by God's grace, can look beyond the limits of the present and envision a future made possible by God: life in abundance.

The Object of Hope Revealed

Christian hope is rooted in the revelation of God to the people Israel, expressed eloquently in the Judaic tradition. This revelation has been passed down through oral tradition and sacred writings. For Jews and Christians alike, this revelation is their most treasured legacy.

Hope for the Exile

In the Hebrew Scriptures, ancient Israel's hope rested entirely on Yahweh. It was Yahweh who provided for their needs, and they held this hope firm because of Yahweh's past deeds. These deeds have been revealed in countless stories found in the Hebrew Scriptures, such as the following:

- Giving them new names, Yahweh blesses and makes a Covenant with Abraham and Sarah (Genesis 15:1–21; 17:3–22).
- By Sarah—made fertile at an advanced age by God—giving birth to Isaac, Yahweh continues to fulfill the Promise (Genesis 21:1–18).
- Finding hope in Yahweh's Promise, Moses leads Israel out of slavery in Egypt (Exodus, chapters 1–16).
- Placing her hope in Elijah's prophecy, the widow of Zarephath prepares her last portion of flour and oil for the prophet Elijah and her son. As a result, they continue to eat for over a year (1 Kings 17:1–16).

For much of their history, the people of Israel lived in exile under the oppressive yoke of foreign rulers. In their exile, hopelessness was not foreign to the Israelites. Yet these stories of exile reveal a living hope that Israel sustained during its captivity—a hope that stubbornly clung to a future time of freedom.

Even while lamenting their exile, the people of Israel cried out to God for relief. However profound their experience of suffering, Israel seized the opportunity for exodus and freedom when it arrived because their present situation was not considered entirely without hope. The story of Israel reveals that though the journey involved times of blurred vision and persistent bickering, their hope endured. If the present had been Isreal's only reality, they could have given in completely to despair.

The significance of hope in Israel's history is that God's revelation came especially to society's marginalized. Hope in Yahweh was the sustaining bread of widows, orphans, and exiles.

Hope's Promise Fulfilled

The fulfillment of God's promise first offered to Abraham and Sarah is fully revealed in Jesus Christ. Through him the Christian has hope for the Reign of God on earth and, ultimately, for his or her own resurrection into eternal blessedness.

And yet, no Gospel writer ever portrays Jesus as demanding hope of his disciples. Jesus encourages faith and exhorts his followers to love, but he never explicitly employs the word *hope*. In Jesus' proclamations of the near yet future Reign of God—life in all its fullness—and in his healing those who suffer, hope is found between the lines. This unspoken hope is the response of the listener to the sound of the following good news:

- The Reign of God is compared to a mustard seed, to a bit of yeast (Luke 13:18–21), and to being both here and yet to come (Luke 17:20–21).
- The Beatitudes offer blessing on those who suffer. Jesus promises consolation, spiritual riches, and peace at a future time. The object of these promises is the Reign of heaven (Matthew 5:1–12; Luke 6:20–23).

19

- The image of the Reign of God as a wedding feast filled with the poor as guests inspires hope (Matthew 22:1–14; Luke 14:12–24).
- In every story, the presentation of the deformed, destitute, and deprived before Christ for healing is not simply a leap of faith, but is also an act of profound hope.
- Most significantly, Jesus' own Resurrection from the dead reveals that God's promise is ultimately fulfilled by doing the impossible—raising Jesus from death to life.
- The coming of the Holy Spirit, the Advocate who dwells with us to bring wisdom, truth, and inspiration, fulfills Christ's promise not to leave us homeless, hopeless orphans.

So Jesus never mentions the need to hope. He is the source of hope to all people, and in the midst of his life, death, and Resurrection, a lively hope abides. In the other books of the Christian Testament, Christ is the ground of hope for every Christian community. It is Jesus who proclaims the near yet future Reign of God on earth. It is Jesus who reveals that this Reign will mean healing the sick and broken, correcting injustice, and ultimately raising all who have died.

Placing our hope in Christ means placing our hope in God's Reign that is a new world of justice, equity, freedom, peace, and well-being. Thus, within our own suffering and death, our hope is the resilient conviction that even amid suffering and tragedy, an overriding purpose prevails: God loves us and has already accomplished the impossible by raising Jesus from the dead. The suffering, death, and Resurrection of Christ can become the horizon within which we interpret our present experience of pain, loss, and failure to love.

The hope of the Jew and Christian has been formed and transformed by God's historical revelation to all people. This revelation of God with us is our most cherished legacy. It is the sustaining bread for our spiritual journey and the reason for our hope. This legacy reveals that we can not only desire but also expect God's love for us and our love for God. The rich biblical tradition reveals that the foundation of hope is love, and in the context of this love, both Jews and Christians wait together in hope for the world that God intends.

Between Presumption and Despair: Hope

The human heart, heavy, winter-frozen, hardened, and cracked, or spring-soaked, flooded, and thawing, lives amid tremendous ambiguity and temptation. We are tempted to take control of this ambiguity by clinging to one of the two extremes of either presumption or despair. Clinging to presumption, one might glare at the face of tragedy and scream, "All depends on God!" Adhering to despair, the desperate declare, "All depends on me!" While both might offer a temporary sense of power, both are inadequate responses to ambiguity. Both relinquish human responsibility and arrest the potentiality of hope. Both are life-denying.

Common to both presumption and despair is a subtle yet pervasive denial of reality. Presumption flees the world and demands that God's grace magically improve earthly conditions. In fitful self-willing and cynicism, despair forgoes the power of God's grace.

The hope of the Christian is the grace-filled mean between presumption and despair. Christian hope takes the middle way, which requires both human will and the grace of God. Christian hope boldly embraces the delicate balance between the expectation of goodness beyond the present woe, the responsibility that must be taken to make the world a livable place, and the intrinsic yet potent grace of God at work in it all.

Christian hope yields to the mean, the way provided by the life that comes out of the death and Resurrection of Jesus. This is the way that asks us to use our power to hope in a future more blessed than broken. At the same time, it invites us to yield to and ask for God's grace to build that future through us. It is a journey that invites us to disclose the hope we have in God by building homes for the homeless or by filling sandbags to hold back a rising river.

The seed that grows is the one that stays firmly planted in the ground. Christians who hope, embrace the ambiguity of the human heart and the planet Earth and plant their roots deep in the good soil of the Gospel promise of Christ: death and sin are conquered, the Advocate is with us to build the Reign of God that will come.

Grief: The Companion of Hope

Many of us have learned more about hope during times when we have been without it. Painful grief burns away fleeting and superficial hope that depends on possessions or on control over life. Perhaps because we fear that grief will lead to despair, we are tempted to leave our losses unnamed and unexpressed, but doing so can leave us cynical or altogether hopeless. Cynicism can become a cover for vulnerability and pain.

Continually bombarded with what is not right with the world or even for our own life, we might ask: What is there to hope for? Did Christ's suffering, death, and Resurrection radically change anything? How can we feed the fire of hope in our heart when our life has been soaked in disappointment? What does my ache and grief have to do with a hope that is in God?

Paradoxically, grieving our losses can deepen our capacity for hope in a new day. The process of remembering, appreciating, reflecting on, and praying on what has been can instruct and remind us of the good that was and can come again. Loss also compels us to seek the face of the loving God who will sustain us in our grieving and healing. Our religious ancestors learned the lessons of hope rising from the ashes of grief. The people Israel grieved the loss of the Temple for two generations before the prophet Isaiah announced a year of favor from the Lord (Isaiah 54:1–3). Psalm 22 laments: "My God, my God, why have you deserted me?" but several lines later declares, "In you our ancestors put their trust; they trusted and you rescued them" (1–4).

The Apostles cowered in fear and grief after Jesus' death. Their grief reminded them of all the love that Jesus had poured out on them. So by the time of the Resurrection and even more so at Pentecost, the hearts of the disciples were open and searching for the fulfillment of God's promise. Thus, when Jesus appeared to the downhearted disciples on the road to Emmaus, their hearts burned within them with fresh power and hope (Luke 24:32).

When Jesus said that he came to bring life in abundance, he did not promise a life without suffering or grief. Grief is a constant companion on the journey of a hopeful life. And grief is an invitation to deeper hope. Without necessary losses and without passing through the grieving that accompanies loss, our hope can become false piety and cheap cliché. Before we are able to embrace the hope at the foundation of our humanity found in Christ, we can progress through our losses layer by layer, often through tears and lamentation.

Hope is more than a superficial wish. Hope is experiencing the highs and lows of daily existence and turning toward tomorrow—setting the losses toward the future. Hope embraces the overwhelming grief of life's default and of dreams gone bankrupt as invitations to empty out the human heart and to fine-tune our hope into its own unique revolt against a world that would have us think that God has forgotten us. Moving through loss allows us to be ready always to enter places we have not yet been. Our future can then include a new hope after the old hope is past and gone. This future is given to all people in Jesus Christ—the one whose life, death, and Resurrection become our freedom and our life.

Other Challenges to Hope

Although the biblical tradition offers a rich landscape for a religious hopefulness, we are living in a culture that too often diminishes the horizon of hope and, therefore, the fullness of life. Rabbi Harold Kushner tells this Hasidic story:

> [A man received] a telegram telling him that a relative had died and left him some valuable property. He was to contact his rabbi for details. Excited, he went to the rabbi, only to be told that the relative was Moses and the valuable property was the Jewish religious tradition. [Upon hearing this, the man went away] disappointed that [the] legacy was religious wisdom and not downtown real estate.

As this story reveals, what we consider valuable and worthy of our hope may not be the same as the treasures of our own religious tradition of hope. In fact, the two may lie in stark contradiction.

Besides presumption, despair, and grief, note these other powerful challenges to the virtue of hope:

"I am what I own." Advertisements tell us that unless we have certain products, we are inadequate, deprived, unacceptable, and probably ugly. Objects are

24

marketed as being necessary for a happy life. We are bombarded with new objects for which to hope. Such materialism and consumerism orient us toward the belief that "I am what I own."

To hope for things is natural. Every person needs some material goods for a safe, healthy, and fulfilling life. Yet years of polling data conclude that increased consumption and wealth have not produced a more hopeful society, a culture that finds hope in a God who has established the dignity of every person.

Immediate gratification. Our culture values instant gratification. We see this in many signs, such as the ever-growing demand for fast food. People are even shot on the freeway for not driving fast enough. The rich dynamism of moving with God's grace gets forgotten in the rush to gratification.

Hope is the radical refusal to let the present time be all that life can offer. It is the unflinching conviction that the future holds positive possibilities. Hopefulness is more than an emotional wishfulness. It is a conscious and sometimes stubbornly determined movement of the imagination and the will toward full life.

"*Noli me tangere.* Touch me not." Another challenge to hope is believing that we can purchase hope on our own terms, independent of the ways in which our decisions and actions influence anyone else. Not only are we told that we should have what we want when we want it, but we are also led to believe that no one else should get in the way. Few products made in sweatshops or by convict labor advertise the facts of their manufacture. But the hope that Christ brings can never be achieved by exploiting other people.

While hope is grounded in the stirring of each heart, Christian hope is not a private affair. It is founded on a common hope of a world community. This means

25

that as one hopes for material goods in order to live well, one must also reflect on how the pursuit of these goods is within or outside of God's Reign, a Reign not simply for oneself but for the entire world. God's promise of a future life in abundance is not just for the individual but for all people and creation. Christian hope is an interdependent hope.

Growing in Hope

Because the virtue of hope is challenged by the temptation to either extreme of presumption or despair, the unavoidable experiences of loss, and some of the values of our culture, we reflect upon and pray for hope. Reflecting on and praying for hope focus our attention on how we hope and what we hope for. Reflecting on and praying about hope nourish the tiny seed of hope that God has planted in our heart. Prayer—a quiet listening and responding to God—looks at the condition of that field and tends the seeds planted there. Reflection and prayer loosen the soil, break up hard clods of dirt, sink the hoe deep into the ground, and shed light and rain. Reflection and prayer prepare the heart for God's grace so that the seed of hope can grow.

Meditating on the passages and stories in this book can help you listen to your heart, examine aspects of how you hope, and plant hopeful moments in your imagination. The reflections also suggest ways of cooperating with God's grace so that you will grow in hope: for example, watching for miracles, taking small steps forward, learning detachment, acting compassionately, sowing a garden.

In the First Letter of Peter, the writer exhorts us, "Always be ready to make your defense to anyone who demands from you an accounting for the hope that is in you" (3:15). As Christians we are summoned by our baptism to bear witness to the radical yet pervasive Reign of God on earth. This Reign, this life in abundance, that is revealed in Jesus Christ, is the reason for our hope. May we grow in hope for Jesus who is the way, the truth, and the life. May our hope in Christ be steadfast and unwearied.

Changed by Hope

Listen

You [God] supremely are that selfsame, for You are not
changed and in You is that rest in which all cares are
forgotten, since there is no other besides You, and we
have not to seek other things which are not what You
are: but You, Lord, alone have *made me dwell in hope.*

(Augustine of Hippo)

◆ ◆ ◆ ◆ ◆

Reflect

Hope changes the heart. Hope offers a proper perspective about our efforts and the priority of our actions, or as Augustine says, "we have not to seek other things which are not what You are." In other words, hopeful hearts do not sweat the small stuff, do not make mountains out of molehills, do not believe that their effort is the only one at work. Those who hope in God accept that their efforts for good are a participation in a whole historical movement toward the good that may or may not be achieved in their lifetime. The future depends on God and not on our efforts alone. God is not changed by our hope, but our heart can be changed when we hope in God.

How has your hope challenged you to let go of the small stuff? What small stuff is weighing you down? What is possible now that once was not? What has your hope made possible?

Respond

God of hopeful hearts, may your grace be enough for me today. May my insecurities be lessened as my hope in you increases. Help me to live in the way that you have made me. Grant peaceful rest to my worries and concerns, that I might rest in you.

Small, Positive Changes

Listen

Every small, positive change we can make in ourselves repays us in confidence in the future.

(Alice Walker)

◆ ◆ ◆ ◆ ◆

ℛeflect

This day is an opportunity to try something new or to make one small, positive change. Maybe try to read some hopeful passage for ten minutes. Maybe pray a morning prayer on the way to work or while on an errand. Maybe cook a new recipe. Maybe consciously let go of an old grudge, or try praising rather than criticizing someone who gets under your skin. In other words, respond to God's grace through some small act of hope. The little, positive changes can open doors not considered before.

Remembering the adage from the foreword, "plant an act, reap a habit," what small, positive change comes to mind? What would you need to do today to make this change?

ℛespond

God of hope, a new day is before me, and I would like to try something new. I believe that hope for a brighter future begins with small, positive changes, acts planted that will turn into hopeful habits. Guide me with wisdom and strength as I try to change this behavior.

Bread of the Exiled

Listen

For surely I know the plans I have for you, says the LORD,
plans for your welfare, and not for harm,
to give you a future with hope.
Then when you call upon me
and come and pray to me,
I will hear you.
When you search for me, you will find me;
if you seek me with all your heart,
I will let you find me, says the LORD.

(Jeremiah 29:11–14)

◆ ◆ ◆ ◆ ◆

Reflect

Jeremiah's words were challenging to a community exiled from Jerusalem and in a spiritual crisis. The people of Israel had been forced from their land and driven into exile in Babylon. The Temple in Jerusalem, the center of their religious practice, had been destroyed. Many of their teachers and priests had been massacred. Strangers in a hostile land, the people of Israel had to pick up the pieces of their lives, reconstitute their religious practice, and re-form their sense of community—or be plunged into despair.

Speaking on God's behalf, the prophet Jeremiah reminds the Israelites that God's future for them is full of hope because it is a future that God will provide. Israel will find God in exile with them. They will eventually return to Jerusalem, but until then they must seek God with all their heart. God will be with them even far from home.

Consider a time in your own life when you have felt exiled or alienated. What did you do to cope with this separation from a beloved person, place, or situation?

Respond

God of the exiled, I place my future in your hands. Your promise and your grace allow me to boldly pray: I do not know where I am going but, in you, I know that I am not lost. Guide my steps along peaceful ways, keep me from harm's way, fill me with hope.

No Right to Despair

Listen

"At this moment, I want to restate my conviction, as a man of hope, that a new ray of salvation will appear. And I want to encourage to the same conviction those who have the goodness to be listening to me. No one has a right to sink into despair. We all have the duty to seek together new channels and to hope actively, as Christians. I believe that these events and these questions put us in need of a pastoral appeal, which is what to me is the meaning of what I am about to say to you: what must be saved before all is our people's march toward liberation. The people have begun a march that has already cost much blood and that must not be wasted. The crisis in this advance must be solved in the success of the advance, and that is what we must seek. Using a comparison from today's gospel [the story of the wise men from the East] we might say that the star that must today guide the people, the government, and the various sectors must be this: how to keep that march of the people toward social justice from becoming stagnant and atrophied, and how to preserve and further it."

(Oscar Romero)

◆ ◆ ◆ ◆ ◆

Reflect

Romero's prophetic words remind us that our hope is part of that ongoing process of transformation that did not begin and does not end with us. In hope we can do what we can to "keep that march of the people toward social justice from becoming stagnant," but we cannot expect to see the end result in our time on earth! We hope in the process of the march, which will not be completed in our lifetime. Christian hope involves creative energy now, but also a healthy detachment and a reliance on the flow of God's grace.

How are you seeking creative channels for hopeful energy? In what area of your life do you need to step back and take the long view?

Respond

Living God, sometimes I get so involved with my work that I forget that you are the master builder. When I try to cling to my own efforts, I can lose sight of your Reign, your vision, and your shalom. Set me on the right course. Make me your prophet for a future yet to be revealed, and fill me with creative energy for justice.

$\mathcal{A}$ Telling Hope

$\mathcal{L}$isten

Now who will harm you if you are eager to do what is good? But even if you do suffer for doing what is right, you are blessed. Do not fear what they fear, and do not be intimidated, but in your hearts sanctify Christ as Lord. Always be ready to make your defense to anyone who demands from you an accounting for the hope that is in you; yet do it with gentleness and reverence.

(1 Peter 3:13–16)

◆ ◆ ◆ ◆ ◆

Reflect

This passage is an encouragement to tell others why we are hopeful: because we are blessed by Christ who stands with us in all circumstances. Perhaps today someone will need us to listen to their struggles. Perhaps today we will need to tell a friend about our own struggles. Gentleness and respect, given to someone or received from someone, can help us to accept where we need to be today.
Whether or not our hope is a consuming fire or a flickering flame, we stoke the fire of hope by gentle and respectful listening.

Reflect on why it is difficult to maintain a sense of hope. What gets in the way? What grace do you need to be more hope filled today instead of fearful or intimidated?

Respond

Loving Jesus, I seek you with my heart. With your grace I shall respond to those around me with gentleness and respect. I now place before you those things that dampen my hopeful spirit. I ask for your grace this day to overcome my fears and anxieties and to celebrate your blessing.

Simplify and See

Listen

Those who abandon everything in order to seek God know well that [God] is the God of the poor.

(Thomas Merton)

◆ ◆ ◆ ◆ ◆

Reflect

The presence and promise of God is more visible to those not obsessed with the acquisition of material wealth. This is not to say that materially poor people should be envied, for poverty itself remains a sad condition. Rather, a sincere and deep level of nonpossessiveness or detachment can leave us unencumbered for the work of God in the world. Those who hope in God and not in power or possessions indeed experience a radical poverty and a radical hope, that is, one that cuts to the root of life's sacred meaning and keeps it in perspective.

Ponder and pray over the following questions: In what areas of my life do I feel insecure? In what way is my life out of perspective? How can I simplify my life today?

Respond

God of the poor, help me to delight in the gifts of your creation and to keep my hope in you. May I see how my insecurities and competitiveness get in the way of placing my hope in you. With your grace I will approach this day with simplicity and hope.

Renewed Each Morning

Listen

My soul is bereft of peace;
    I have forgotten what happiness is;
so I say, "Gone is my glory,
    and all that I had hoped for from the LORD."

The thought of my affliction and my homelessness
    is wormwood and gall!
My soul continually thinks of it
    and is bowed down within me.
But this I call to mind,
    and therefore I have hope:

The steadfast love of the LORD never ceases,
    [God's] mercies never come to an end;
they are new every morning;
    great is your faithfulness.
"The LORD is my portion," says my soul,
    "therefore I will hope in [God]."

(Lamentations 3:17–24)

◆ ◆ ◆ ◆ ◆

Reflect

At the time of Jesus Christ's arrest, two of his disciples suffered because of what one had done and what the other had failed to do. Both Judas Iscariot and Simon Peter compromised their loyalty to Jesus: one by turning Jesus in to the authorities, the other by denying his relationship to Jesus three times. By these actions both had cause for heart-wrenching regret. Both could have recited these verses from the Book of Lamentations. And yet one disciple did not despair of God's mercy and the other disciple did. The next morning, as one was hanging from a tree, the other, who would eventually be known as the rock, renewed his hope and returned to Jesus.

Reflect on your own acts of disloyalty, betrayal, and moral cowardice. Do you still stand in need of forgiveness? Do you need to offer it? Remember that the mercy of God is made new each day. Offer your own lamentations. Ask God for forgiveness and the hope to carry on in divine love.

Respond

God of mercy and forgiveness, sometimes I have made big mistakes. Forgive me and help me to remember that I can always turn to you. Let me always recall that my hope is not only about the future but also about your forgiveness and love.

Asikhatali

Listen

Asikhatali noma si boshwa
Sizimisel' inkululeko
Unzima lomthwalo
Ufuna madoda

It doesn't matter if you should jail us
We are free and kept alive by hope
Our struggle's hard
But vict'ry will
Restore our lands
To our hands

(South African spiritual)

◆ ◆ ◆ ◆ ◆

Reflect

The witness of spiritual strength given to us by the
people who struggled against apartheid in South Africa
inspired awe. For centuries native South Africans have
been subjected to an apartheid system where people's
possibilities and future depended entirely on the color of
their skin. Despite generations of oppression, many of
the people of South Africa did not give up their songs.
As Susan Robeson wrote, "They sang to forget the chains
and misery. The sorrow will one day turn to joy. All that
breaks the heart and oppresses the soul will one day give
place to peace and understanding, and every[one] will be
free." The music kept hope alive despite the oppressive
system.

What oppresses you? What would deny your hope?
Amid your own struggle for liberation, what song can
you sing? What lyrics and melody offer hope to your life?
Sing a song of hope.

Respond

Liberating God, you intend that all people should be free
in your sight. I wish to see all people as you see them.
Help me to free my sister and brother by listening to
their voices and by joining in their song. May we sing
together your one song of salvation.

Ash Wednesday

Listen

What is humanity?
Hope turned to dust?
No. Humanity is dust turned to hope.

(Elie Wiesel)

Reflect

Each year on the first day of the Paschal season, Christians worldwide are signed with a cross of ashes on their forehead: *"Memento homo, quia pulvis es, et in pulverum reverteris"*—"Remember that you are dust, and to dust you shall return." This cross, the most powerful symbol of Ash Wednesday, reminds us of Christ's ultimate victory over death. Because of Christ's Resurrection, our humanity is turned to life instead of death, to hope instead of ash.

And yet Elie Wiesel wrote his words as a Jewish survivor of the Nazi concentration camps, not as a Christian praying on Ash Wednesday. After the Holocaust, two-thirds of European Jews had been killed as part of Hiter's "Final Solution." The smoke and ashes of the crematoriums were testament to the extermination of real people that daily posed the question, "What is humanity? Hope turned to dust?" Who could see the smoke in the sky and feel the ash in the air and still hope?

For both Jews and Christians, ashes represent what is horrendous about prejudiced human action and what is possible and redeemable through a God who, contrary to all the monstrous deeds of human beings, is a God of love, justice, and compassion. Remember that for one people the ashes are a reminder of sin that has been

♦ ♦ ♦ ♦ ♦

overcome, so they should live as children of light. For
others the ashes are a reminder of the adversity their
people have had to overcome and of the power of their
hope in God, so they should live as children of hope.
What is your experience of hope in the ashes?

Respond

Loving God, blessed be your many names. Forgive me
my sins as I forgive those who have sinned against me.
Help me to acknowledge the sin of my prejudice and to
transform my mind and heart to openness and accep-
tance of others. Help me to take this hopeful step toward
your holy Reign.

Sweet Wisdom

Listen

My child, eat honey, for it is good,
    and the drippings of the honeycomb are sweet to
        your taste.
Know that wisdom is such to your soul;
    if you find it, you will find a future,
    and your hope will not be cut off.

(Proverbs 24:13–14)

◆ ◆ ◆ ◆ ◆

Reflect

More and more people are recovering the ancient process of making wine at home. Sugar, water, yeast, and a favorite fruit specially treated produce new wine. Yet the best wines are those that have had the time to age and mature.

Wisdom is like wine, and information is like the ingredients. Today human beings are not short on information. Up-to-the-minute news, weather, and sports are available twenty-four hours a day. Internet web sites make international information exchange possible from the living room in one's home. With all of this information, is the human race becoming more wise? Immediate information is not wisdom, for wisdom is information that has matured through a process of reflection, prayer, and study. It becomes a cause for hopefulness when it has had time to mix with these ingredients. Perhaps this explains why Thomas Merton proclaimed his preference for stale news at the abbey. In his opinion, news that was a month or two late had a point to it. Hope draws off of wisdom as its treasured account.

Reflect on the difference between information and wisdom. In what ways might you become caught up in information overload? How has hope been your source of wisdom?

Respond

Holy Wisdom, I live in a world bombarded by information. And I do not know that I am truly becoming wise. Help me to discern and sift through what I know so that I may become a wiser and more hopeful person.

Convicted of Hope?

Listen

Miguel Unamuno
insists that if you want to know
what [someone's] real faith is,
you must find out
not what he says he believes
but what he really hopes for.

The object of our hope
gives clearer indication
of our relationship to biblical faith
than what we do on Sunday morning,

. . . .

What do we hope for?

. . . .

Is it for the kind
of terrible and responsible freedom
that comes from living in a defatalized world—
the world in which God
has handed the reins over to us
and won't come down from the cross
even to save himself?
Do we hope for this,
or for something less demanding?

(Harvey Cox)

◆ ◆ ◆ ◆ ◆

Reflect

Unamuno's commentary is a challenge that cuts to the heart. With the hectic pace of everyday life, it is helpful to take a step back to look at where we are heading. At this moment, where is our hope directed? How do we spend our time? It is one thing to answer these two questions and quite another to actually examine the activities of our day. We might say what we hope for, but if we look at our schedule and where the pockets of anxiety hide, we may discover something new about the object of our hope.

Spend some time today reflecting on your schedule. Perhaps make a time line on paper and write in your activities. Notice whether your activities actually reveal what you hope for and where you hope to go. Then ask yourself: How do I manifest hope to people in need by my actions as well as in my prayers? Can I see in my family life, recreation, and work, contributions to God's Reign of peace?

Respond

God, my eternal shalom, may your gift of peace be the constant in all my activities today. Even if I become fragmented by competing demands on my time and energy, help me to be a person of peace today. Help me to live a responsible and active hope.

Suffering, Endurance, Character

Listen

Therefore, since we are justified by faith,
we have peace with God through our Lord Jesus Christ,
through whom we have obtained access
to this grace in which we stand;
and we boast in our hope of sharing the glory of God.
And not only that, but we also boast in our sufferings,
knowing that suffering produces endurance,
and endurance produces character,
and character produces hope,
and hope does not disappoint us,
because God's love has been poured into our hearts
through the Holy Spirit that has been given to us.

(Romans 5:1–5)

◆ ◆ ◆ ◆ ◆

Reflect

During periods of personal struggle and intense suffering, remember Paul's progression toward hope described in his Letter to the Romans. The movement from suffering to endurance to character to hope depends on God's grace. How suffering leads to hope is rooted in Christ's own suffering, death, and Resurrection. For Jesus is the way through which our own struggle can be understood.

When have you experienced suffering that led to the development of your character? What happened? Were there times when you did not feel that the suffering was fruitful? Or when you did experience grace in the midst of or through the suffering?

Respond

God of light and peace, I cannot change my suffering to hope on my own, nor is it easy to hope while I am suffering. I depend on you and your grace to bring my suffering to an abiding, joy-filled hope. Into your loving hands, I place my struggle and pain with . . .

Jericho Road

Listen

A true revolution of values will soon cause us to question the fairness and justice of many of our past and present policies. On the one hand we are called to play the Good Samaritan on life's roadside; but that will be only an initial act. One day we must come to see that the whole Jericho Road must be transformed so that men and women will not be constantly beaten and robbed as they make their journey on life's highway. True compassion is more than flinging a coin to a beggar; it is not haphazard and superficial. It comes to see that an edifice which produces beggars needs restructuring. A true revolution of values will soon look uneasily on the glaring contrast of poverty and wealth.

(Martin Luther King Jr.)

◆ ◆ ◆ ◆ ◆

Reflect

We are called to be good Samaritans on the Jericho Road. Every person we meet, especially those who stand outside the status quo, should confront our comfort and complacency. Am I the Christian on the Jericho road? Do I fling coins to the "beggars," that is, do I give those who ask a few minutes here or there, so that I can be on my way? True compassion is more than conscience-soothing almsgiving. True compassion considers the whole person and her or his future. It aches for those robbed by unjust policies. It examines the system's effects on the person and the future. True compassion goes beyond a private hope and seeks the hope of the community and its future.

Take time to do an examen of conscience, talking with God about this question: How am I helping to create the Reign of the just and compassionate God for all my sisters and brothers?

Respond

God of compassion, when I consider all the world's ills and those directly affected by unjust systems, I become overwhelmed. Dr. King hoped for the transformation of the "ism" society, but thirty years have passed since he declared his dream, and people are still robbed and beaten on the Jericho Road. Open my eyes to see how I can make the road safer for others. Give me courage and hope to examine current policies and systems with the values of Jesus.

Can't Always Tell by Lookin'

Listen

Under a sky the color of pea soup
she is looking at her work growing away there
actively, thickly like grapevines or pole beans
as things grow in the real world, slowly enough.
If you tend them properly, if you mulch, if you water,
if you provide birds that eat insects a home and winter
    food,
if the sun shines and you pick off caterpillars,
if the praying mantis comes and the ladybugs and the
    bees,
then the plants flourish, but at their own internal clock.
Connections are made slowly, sometimes they grow
    underground.
You cannot tell always by looking what is happening.
More than half a tree is spread out in the soil under your
    feet.
Penetrate quietly as the earthworm that blows no
    trumpet.
Fight persistently as the creeper that brings down the
    tree.
Spread like the squash plant that overruns the garden.
Gnaw in the dark and use the sun to make sugar.
Weave real connections, create real nodes, build real
    houses.
Live a life you can endure: make love that is loving.
Keep tangling and interweaving and taking more in,
a thicket and bramble wilderness to the outside but to us
interconnected with rabbit runs and burrows and lairs.

Live as if you liked yourself, and it may happen:
reach out, keep reaching out, keep bringing in.

◆ ◆ ◆ ◆ ◆

This is how we are going to live for a long time: not
    always,
for every gardener knows that after the digging, after the
    planting,
after the long season of tending and growth, the harvest
    comes.

(Marge Piercy)

Reflect

Raising crops and raising children can be great acts of
hope. One hopeful act feeds the world, the other offers
the world its future. One cannot tell always by looking
what is happening. Parenthood and farming: dramatic
acts of hope.

Reflect on your relationship with your children or
with children you know. Spend some time with children.
Reflect on growing a garden as an act of hope. Plant seeds!

Respond

O Nurturing Parent, help us to be good, hopeful garden-
ers of your children and your earth.

A Feared Reality

Listen

Hope is the most feared reality of any oppressive system. More powerful than any other weapon, hope is the great enemy of those who would control history. What salvation events bring to the world, most of all, is hope, and the world's oppressed peoples are always the ones who have the most at stake in them.

(Jim Wallis)

◆ ◆ ◆ ◆ ◆

Reflect

Recent history reveals salvation events: the end of apartheid, the fall of communism, the seat in the front of the bus taken by Rosa Parks in Montgomery, Alabama, and so on. For each of these salvation events, someone had hope. Someone looked at what had been and would not accept that history was closed and fixed. That hope focused on the possibility of impossibility, a kind of hope that is an energy of transformation. As Jim Wallis says, "Hope is the door from one reality to another."

Reflect on what has looked like it could never happen, but did. When have you hoped in spite of the evidence? As you anticipate the future, what looks impossible but might be changed by hope?

Respond

God of justice, hope is the door to change. Give us the eyes of hope. Show us the door. Grant us the courage to enter this doorway, to envision a world no longer able to live without justice and compassion. Help us to bear the cost of possibilities, whatever they might be. Through the hope you have given us, may the world be transformed.

Tested in Fire

Listen

My child, when you come to serve the Lord,
    prepare yourself for testing.
Set your heart right and be steadfast,
    and do not be impetuous in time of calamity.
Cling to [God], . . .
    so that your last days may be prosperous.
Accept whatever befalls you,
    and in times of humiliation be patient.
For gold is tested in the fire,
    and those found acceptable, in the furnace of
        humiliation.
Trust in [God], and [God] will help you;
    make your ways straight, and hope in [God].

(Sirach 2:1–6)

◆ ◆ ◆ ◆ ◆

Reflect

According to the prophet, trials are not only unavoidable, they are to be expected. No manner of life is without worry, no decision made with absolute certainty. No philosophy answers all the questions, no level of education offers full knowledge. Commitments of all kinds require steadfastness in uncertainty and the discipline of self-sacrifice. Here the prophet reminds us that our trust and our hope in God can protect us in the furnace. All commitments, however grand or small, can be sustained by a daily turning to God, entrusting the day and our future.

In the quiet hours of the early morning or late evening, reflect on the commitments that need to be kept or have been kept today. Are some of your commitments more difficult to keep than others? Were you able or unable to keep them today? Ask God for the grace to be steadfast in these commitments.

Respond

Loving God, I offer to you this day each of my many commitments. May your grace of steadfastness and patience be with me when I am tested. I ask especially for perseverance in hope for the following commitment(s) . . .

Help me to be faithful, loving, and kind.

A Historied Hope

Listen

The world is not yet finished,
but is understood as engaged in a history.
It is therefore the world of possibilities,
the world in which we can serve the future,
promised truth and righteousness and peace.
This is an age of diaspora,
of sowing in hope, of self-surrender and sacrifice,
for it is an age which stands within the horizon
of a new future.

(Jurgen Moltmann)

◆ ◆ ◆ ◆ ◆

Reflect

The events of this day are invitations to hope. We are a
people of the diaspora, scattered lives with unfinished
histories. Each of us is invited to do as Jesus would, wherever this day takes us. With every hope-filled act, we are
planting a future that is not yet seen.

Look for the invitations to hope that come from
widows, strangers, and orphans today. What sacrifice can
you make today for this "age which stands within the
horizon of a new future"?

Respond

God of eternity, sometimes it is difficult to answer the
invitation to hope. In fact, it is easy to forget my call to
be an instrument of hope for my family and friends, let
alone for refugees and immigrants or the widows and
orphans mentioned in the Scriptures. Open my heart to
the experience of those who are scattered and far from
home. Open my eyes to the invitations to hope today.

This Too Shall Pass

Listen

"You will forget your misery;
    you will remember it as waters that have passed
        away.
And your life will be brighter than the noonday;
    its darkness will be like the morning.
And you will have confidence, because there is hope;
    you will be protected and take your rest in safety.
You will lie down, and no one will make you afraid."

(Job 11:16–19)

ℛeflect

Every day, no matter how productive, contains some degree of incompleteness. Every human being, no matter how gifted, is touched by some form of suffering. Every lifetime passes through periods of misery. Each period of profound darkness will have an element of despair and uncertainty: Will this darkness pass? Is this darkness a place of life or a place of death? Maybe bats and mushrooms like the darkness, but I do not.

The Book of Job reminds us that we might think about these periods as waters that will pass, forceful waves that will submerge a sense of well-being and happiness for a time. Hope is the grace to experience misery without deadening finality, as water and womb for growth and life, rather than as a tomb. Talk with God about the words from Job.

ℛespond

Loving God, sometimes the waters of anxiety and pain rise too high around me. Divide these waters as Moses parted the Red Sea, so that I may pass to greater freedom. Quiet the storm and still the waves as Jesus calmed the Sea of Galilee, that I may find restful sleep. In these times I know that you are with me. You are my hope.

The Mystery of Suffering

Listen

But we have something deeper and more valuable to give you, the only truth capable of answering the mystery of suffering and of bringing you relief without illusion, and that is faith and union . . . with Christ the Son of God. Christ did not do away with suffering. He did not even wish to unveil entirely the mystery of suffering. He took suffering upon himself and this is enough to make you understand all its value. All of you who feel heavily the weight of the cross, you who are poor and abandoned, you who weep, you who are persecuted for justice, you who are ignored, you the unknown victims of suffering, take courage. You are the preferred children of the kingdom of God, the kingdom of hope, happiness, and life. You are the [sisters and] brothers of the suffering Christ, and with him, if you wish, you are saving the world.

(Vatican Council II)

◆ ◆ ◆ ◆ ◆

Reflect

The word *revelation* originates from the Latin *velum*, meaning "veil," and the Greek *kalymma*, meaning "to remove." Revelation literally means the removal of the veil. Interestingly, the authors of Matthew, Mark, and Luke each relate that at the moment of Jesus' death, the veil in the Temple was torn in two. The veil in the Temple divided God's dwelling place in the ark of the Covenant from the place where the people gathered and prayed. The veil physically separated God from Israel. Thus, to say that at the moment of Christ's death the veil was rent in two was to suggest that in Christ one had seen God and the Covenant had been revealed.

While Christ is the answer to the mystery of suffering, the power and transformation in human suffering is part of the ongoing revelation of Christ in the modern world. This is the message of hope: in the known and unknown victims of suffering is revealed the inbreaking of God's Reign on earth. And in this mystery, the church is not only called to be prophetic by offering hope for the future but also to be pastoral by offering hope today.

Who do you know who is truly suffering around you? Who do you imagine are the unknown victims of suffering? How can you offer a message of hope?

Respond

God of the suffering, in situations where I do not know what to do to alleviate suffering, show me the way. In every experience of this day, may I maintain a sense of awe and respect for your grace at work to bring hope to the world.

A Response to the Word

Listen

"Blessed are the poor in spirit, for theirs is the kingdom of heaven.

"Blessed are those who mourn, for they will be comforted.

"Blessed are the meek, for they will inherit the earth.

"Blessed are those who hunger and thirst for righteousness, for they will be filled.

"Blessed are the merciful, for they will receive mercy.

"Blessed are the pure in heart, for they will see God.

"Blessed are the peacemakers, for they will be called children of God.

"Blessed are those who are persecuted for righteousness' sake, for theirs is the kingdom of heaven.

"Blessed are you when people revile you and persecute you and utter all kinds of evil against you falsely on my account. Rejoice and be glad, for your reward is great in heaven, for in the same way they persecuted the prophets who were before you."

(Matthew 5:3–12)

◆ ◆ ◆ ◆ ◆

Reflect

Unlike the direct challenges to love and to faith, the Gospels do not offer one instance where Jesus calls people to hope. And yet hope is our living response to receiving the stories and the message of the Reign of God. The Beatitudes are an encouragement to hope. They tell us that our present efforts to be and to do the good are connected to a future promised by God. Hope connects this present day to a day that is not yet seen.

    Read the Beatitudes again. Notice which of these hopeful phrases speaks to your heart today. If you are in a time of grieving, let the message, "Blessed are those who mourn, for they will be comforted," be a source of hope. If your heart is cluttered, pray, "Blessed are the pure in heart, for they will see God." Carry one of these Beatitudes in your heart, and repeat it regularly throughout the day.

Respond

Jesus, in the Beatitudes you show your love to your people. You promise them that the present times belong to a future blessing. To these blessings I respond with hope. In you my life has a future.

The Little Bird

Listen

"Hope" is the thing with feathers—
that perches in the soul—
And sings the tune without the words—
And never stops—at all—

And sweetest—in the Gale—is heard—
And sore must be the storm—
That could abash the little Bird—
That kept so many warm—

I've heard it in the chillest land—
And on the strangest Sea—
Yet, never, in Extremity,
It asked a crumb—of Me.

(Emily Dickinson)

◆ ◆ ◆ ◆ ◆

Reflect

Hope, the winged creature, can take us beyond the ordinary day and make it part of the larger course of life. It can lift us up and put us back down into this day with a renewed perspective. The life within is as rich as the life without, for hope rests and withstands the strongest storm at sea. This metaphor describes the transcendent power hope offers us.

Over what anxieties and concerns do you need a broader perspective? What current pressures or storms try to abash this "little Bird"? When, though in "the chillest land" or on "the strangest Sea," have you heard its sweet tune? Sing your own song of hope.

Respond

God of nature and of little birds, may I listen to the sweet song of hope today. When I am running, frazzled and fragmented, may I return to hope's small but continuous song within my soul. May I also be like this winged creature—a hopeful presence—to all I will meet today.

Groaning with Pains of Labor

Listen

I consider that the sufferings of this present time are not worth comparing with the glory about to be revealed to us. For the creation waits with eager longing for the revealing of the children of God; for the creation was subjected to futility, not of its own will but by the will of the one who subjected it, in hope that the creation itself will be set free from its bondage to decay and will obtain the freedom of the glory of the children of God. We know that the whole creation has been groaning in labor pains until now; and not only the creation, but we ourselves, who have the first fruits of the Spirit, groan inwardly while we wait for adoption, the redemption of our bodies. For in hope we were saved. Now hope that is seen is not hope. For who hopes for what is seen? But if we hope for what we do not see, we wait for it with patience.

(Romans 8:18–25)

◆ ◆ ◆ ◆ ◆

Reflect

Christian hope and the demands of daily life exist in some tension. While we await the end of suffering and the beginning of eternal life in Christ, we can be subjected to futility. In Israel, a bus is bombed. In India, an earthquake takes the lives of thousands. In the United States, thousands lose homes in spring floods. As we live through these tragedies, we are a community that groans inwardly. Yet we wait in hope for things to be set right, to be set free from decay. Exactly how this freedom will happen, we cannot be sure. But we hope for what we cannot see.

Read the newspaper or watch the television news. Look for signs of the "groaning pains of labor" of our world. Form a prayer for these pains and the victims of these tragedies today.

Respond

God of promise, while I live in a world that you have set free, the pain of disaster and suffering continues. In fact, it is easier to despair than to hope during these times. Therefore I will place my hope in your promise—for a future I do not see. You are with me.

Fortresses

Listen

I've learned of life this bitter truth
Hope not between the crumbling walls
Of man's gratitude to find repose,
But rather,
Build within thy own soul
Fortresses!

(Georgia Douglas Johnson)

◆ ◆ ◆ ◆ ◆

Reflect

Jesus urges us not to become obsessed with material things. Those things we *must* have eventually have us. To hope simply for material wealth is to build our future between walls that will crumble. Yet if we live from the soul—acting justly, loving tenderly, and walking humbly with God (Micah 6:8)—we can enjoy a lasting happiness and peace.

In what ways have your hopes been between "crumbling walls"? How might you uniquely respond to the instructions, "act justly, love tenderly, and walk humbly with God" today?

Respond

Christ, my gentle friend, you once said, "'where your treasure is, there your heart will be also'" (Matthew 6:21). Open my eyes to see how I overemphasize material possessions, and open my heart to discover ways of justice, humility, and love. May I prepare for the future—build a fortress within my soul—by strengthening my relationships.

Dear Hope

Listen

Like the deer that yearns
for running streams,
so my soul is yearning
for you, my God.
My soul is thirsting for God, the living God.
When can I enter to see the face of God?
. . . .
Why are you so sad, my soul?
Why sigh within me?
Hope in God;
for I will yet praise my savior and my God.

(Psalm 42:1–5)

◆ ◆ ◆ ◆ ◆

Reflect

While in graduate school, I learned a lot about the virtue of hope by sitting near Lake Sagatagan rather than reading volumes of Thomas Aquinas in the library. In the earliest hours of the day, at least an hour before the bells called the monks to prayer, I would hike out to the woods and sit quietly along the lakeshore.

The reason I did this routinely was because of what had occurred there once. I heard what at first sounded like a very odd gurgling. Looking around quietly in the direction of the sound, I saw a fawn along the shore, head bent down, drinking. In the quiet, an explosion of light happened inside me. In that marvelous moment, I experienced the greatness of the Creator who made such beautiful animals to drink from lakeshores. I was out in the woods seeing hope.

Take a walk outdoors today. If this is not possible, remember a time when an act of nature brought your heart to its knees. Experience this time again in your imagination, and realize that your own expectation is indeed an act of hope in the Creator.

Respond

God of waters and fawns, my heart waits to be filled by you. Refresh me with your power and grandeur found in the simplicity and solitude of nature. Open my eyes to see all creation with wonder and hope. Quench my thirst so that nothing can take me away from you. Let me wait in joyful hope for the ways in which you will reveal your face to me this day.

A Mentoring Hope

Listen

We never lost hope despite the segregated world of this rural town because we had adults who gave us a sense of a future—and black folk had an extra lot of problems, and we were taught that we could struggle and change them.

(Marian Wright Edelman)

◆ ◆ ◆ ◆ ◆

Reflect

Those who know us, who believe in us, and who give us wisdom offer us a sense of a future. Mentors help us discover hope and possibility in ourselves and in our world. It is easy to get weighed down in the responsibilities of becoming a new parent, starting a new job, or embarking on a new venture. Those who have been through similar challenges can walk with us and provide guidance and hope when we simply cannot see it.

Who have been and are now significant mentors in your life? What did each one teach you? For whom are you a mentor? How do you offer a sense of hope, a sense of a future, to this person?

Respond

God of wisdom, you sent me the greatest model for my life, Jesus Christ. Through him I am shown the way, the truth, and the life. Thank you for his life and presence with me. Thank you for my mentors, and help me to be an example of hope to others.

We Are Not Lost

Listen

My Lord God, I have no idea where I am going. I do not
see the road ahead of me. I cannot know for certain
where it will end. Nor do I really know myself, and the
fact that I think I am following your will does not mean
that I am actually doing so. But I believe that the desire
to please you does in fact please you. And I hope I have
that desire in all that I am doing. I hope that I will never
do anything apart from that desire. And I know that if I
do this you will lead me by the right road, though I may
know nothing about it. Therefore I will trust you always
though I may seem to be lost and in the shadow of death.
I will not fear, for you are ever with me, and you will
never leave me to face my perils alone.

(Thomas Merton)

Reflect

Merton expresses sincere trust and hope in a future that God will supply. This future is one that he may know nothing about. Here is the sincere act of hope: to place one's future in God's hands and to embrace the ambiguity of the present time with all its pressures and decisions.

Ponder this question: What area of my life do I need to offer to God in hope? Reread Merton's prayer slowly. Let it be an expression of your own hope and trust in God.

Respond

Faithful God, by your grace I place my future in your care. With my hope in you, I may not know where I am going, but I know that I am not lost.

Small White Stones

Listen

Hopes are white stones shining up from the bottom of pools, and every clear day we reach in up to the shoulder, selecting a few and rearranging others, drawing our arms smoothly back into air, leaving no scar on the water.

(Natalie Kusz)

◆ ◆ ◆ ◆ ◆

Reflect

As we begin a new day, we can take a few minutes for quiet reflection. We can look at these small white stones of hope and make adjustments and changes. At the kitchen table, on the bus, in the car, or even before a bowl of cereal, we can enjoy the quality of quiet time and little miracles.

What activities lie before you? What plans or projects do you have to complete? Who will you see today? What small miracles are here now?

Respond

God of the future, slow me down to live for today. Direct my plans as you desire, and help me to let go of unnecessary worry about the future. In these quiet moments, I become anchored in you, my hope.

Risky and Steep

Listen

Who shall ascend into the hill of the Lord? or who shall stand in his holy place? There is no one but us. There is no one to send, nor a clean hand, nor a pure heart on the face of the earth, nor in the earth, but only us, a generation comforting ourselves with the notion that we have come at an awkward time, that our innocent fathers are all dead—as if innocence had ever been—and our children busy and troubled, and we ourselves unfit, not yet ready, having each of us chosen wrongly, made a false start, failed, yielded to impulse and the tangled comfort of pleasures, and grown exhausted, unable to seek the thread, weak, and involved. But there is no one but us. There never has been.

(Annie Dillard)

◆ ◆ ◆ ◆ ◆

Reflect

An old adage declares, "I was waiting for someone to do something, and then I realized that I was someone." It is easier to wait for someone else to initiate change or to make excuses not to become involved with justice. If we are self-doubting, we can find excuses to stay put. We can also talk ourselves out of the steep climb of justice by simply believing that it is too huge a task for our tiny hands. Unfortunately, the action of hoping is diminished by self-doubt.

In what area of your life do you need to be more initiating? Are you waiting for someone else to begin? What small, hopeful step can you make today?

Respond

Gentle God, this day is your gift to me. I know we each have hills before us, and I want to act responsibly with mine. Grant me the wisdom to discover what action to take and the courage to take that step. I ask this in the name of Jesus who took so many risks.

Wildflowers

Listen

SEED. There are so many beginnings. In Japan, I recall, there were wildflowers that grew in the far, cool region of mountains. The bricks of Hiroshima, down below, were formed of clay from these mountains, and so the walls of houses and shops held the dormant trumpet flower seeds. But after one group of humans killed another with the explosive power of life's smallest elements split wide apart, the mountain flowers began to grow. Out of the crumbled, burned buildings they sprouted. Out of destruction and bomb heat and the falling of walls, the seeds opened up and grew. What a horrible beauty, the world going its own way, growing without us. But perhaps this, too, speaks of survival, of hope beyond our time.

(Linda Hogan)

◆ ◆ ◆ ◆ ◆

Reflect

Even when great destruction has occurred among human beings during war, creation keeps going. Seeds do not know about bombs. They will grow if given the opportunity wherever they can break through the earth. Though it cannot be proven, it seems that the natural world, the world of seeds and flowers especially, is evidence of God's hope in us. So great is God's hope, that life comes out of death. So even if some human beings are bent on destruction, God's hope will help the world to grow on.

Reflect on God's hope in humanity, a hope beyond our time. Remember that however great the destruction, God's plan is life, growth, and a future. Repeatedly pray the phrase, "God's plan is life."

Respond

God, creator of wildflowers, you reveal signs that you desire a future for the world. Even though I can become misguided, distrustful, and controlling, you weave your grace and your goodness through me. May I honor and return the hope that you have held for me.

Thy Kingdom Come

Listen

I make this pledge to my people, the dead and the living—to all Americans, black and white. I will not retire nor will I retreat, not one inch, so long as God gives me vision to see what is happening and strength to fight for the things I know are right. For I know that my kingdom, my people's kingdom and the kingdom of all the peoples of all the world, is not beyond the skies, the moon and the stars, but right here at our feet.

(Charlotta Bass)

◆ ◆ ◆ ◆ ◆

Reflect

In 1952, Charlotta Bass made this pledge as the U.S. vice-presidential candidate of the Progressive party. In the Book of Proverbs is the saying, "Where there is no vision, the people perish" (29:18). A society needs leaders who have vision and prophets who remind people of that vision. Although they often lose their life, prophets hold a life-giving role in any culture. They remind us that the Reign of God exists not only outside our world but also in our midst. Whenever we challenge the "isms" of our day—racism, classism, ageism, consumerism—we bring the Reign of God closer to home.

Who have been prophets for you? Who has given you a vision or reminded you of your hope and your dreams? When have you acted prophetically, hopefully?

Respond

Loving God, you are the voice of the prophets, and your Reign of love and justice is one I hope for and seek this day. By your grace I will try to be loving and fair. Help me to speak the truth in love as well as to listen to the truth of the prophets around me. May your Reign come.

Toward the Last Day

Listen

Let us hold fast to the confession of our hope without
wavering, for [Christ] who has promised is faithful. And
let us consider how to provoke one another to love and
good deeds, not neglecting to meet together, as is the
habit of some, but encouraging one another, and all the
more as you see the Day approaching.

(Hebrews 10:23–25)

◆ ◆ ◆ ◆ ◆

Reflect

We will encounter and embrace hope for many good
things, but our hope for health, happiness, and prosperity is only a participation in the ultimate hope that we
have in God. Against endless temptations to despair, we
are called to take the narrow road, that is, to maintain
our hope in God revealed in Jesus Christ. We hold fast to
God in hope not because it is easy but because God will
not disappoint us. It is our vocation on earth, whatever
our particular lifestyle, to evoke in one another this kind
of hope in God that seeks justice, loves deeply, leads to
joy, but does not ignore pain. This hope is what human
beings are called to until the Last Day.

Respond

My God.
As you have promised—
sustain me that I may live;
disappoint me not in my hope.

(Psalm 119:115–116)

Titles in the Life in Abundance series

Growing in Courage by Peter Gilmour
Growing in Hope by Lou Anne M. Tighe
Growing in Joy by Robert F. Morneau

Order from your local bookstore or from
Saint Mary's Press
702 Terrace Heights
Winona, MN 55987-1320
USA
1-800-533-8095

Jesus said, . . . "I came that [you] may have life, and have it
abundantly." (John 10:7–10)

Jesus' mission is accomplished in each one of us when we nourish
the seeds of full life that God has planted in the garden of our soul.